WE WALK BESIDE YOU™

Animal Insights for Everyday Living

Sandra Mendelson

Author of: **WE WALK BESIDE YOU**
Animal Messages for an Awakening World

Cover Illustration by Farlish Mohamed

Book Design by Deana Riddle

We cannot reveal all in a moment.

Our story – the why, how and who we are, must unfurl slowly,

like a flower.

We can only show you snippets of our world at a time.

It would be too much for humans to digest, otherwise.

The leap to understanding that we are intelligent,

intentional beings

with a complex understanding of energy, behavior

and the purpose of life

will send most people's heads reeling.

– Mandrill

What we share with you is metered out:

First, there is exposure.

Then repetition.

Then assimilation into your consciousness.

We don't expect you to change overnight; neither should you.

Repeat what you learn over and over again

to combat forgetfulness.

-Horse (Honeybee)

MEDITATION FROM THE ANIMALS

Close your eyes.

We do not believe what we see. You humans do.

If we did, we would give up.

Close your eyes.

Forget what you see and hear.

What your eyes and ears tell you is already shaped by your beliefs, and those of society.

These beliefs are programmed into you and lie within you.

These beliefs create boundaries between us.

Close your eyes.

Feel the One Heart: Yours, Ours.

Receive with your heart;

it is the one place where you understand

that we are all equal and without limits.

It is only through your heart that you will recognize

what we have been trying to show humans throughout history.

TABLE OF CONTENTS

INTRODUCTION

Since *We Walk Beside You: Animal Messages for an Awakening World* was published in 2017, readers across the globe have written to share their profound experiences of awakening and self-discovery after opening to animal consciousness. I am pleased and delighted to learn that the book continues to inspire and motivate readers to spend more time in stillness in the natural world, and to interact with non-humans from a space of equality and focused attention. As a result of their continued and growing practice, many readers report that they have an increased understanding of—and compassion for—animals. Some have even discovered their own innate abilities to receive information from beyond the five senses and are viewing their life journeys through a lens of deeper meaning.

The wisdom of animals continues to fill me with awe. After nearly a decade of channeling animal consciousness and communicating with individual animals from more than 80 species, my astonishment and admiration for the depth of animal perception, intention, and insight is more vivid than ever. You could say I've been piecing together an everlasting jigsaw puzzle. It will never be completed because, as a human, I will always peer at the inner lives of animals from the outside. In addition, regardless of any animal communicator's gift, receiving all the information and wisdom collectively held by all animals will never be possible. Depending on the fragments the animals choose to reveal to me, I share as much as I can, hoping to form an image that reflects the richness of animal existence.

For readers of this book who are new to the concept of animal consciousness, I offer the following to provide answers to questions that may arise, in order to ensure a rich and rewarding experience as you read:

1. Animal lives are as unique as ours, so generalizations will never encompass all experiences. For example, while all souls incarnated as dogs may share many common behaviors, they can demonstrate shockingly different responses to the same circumstances. Each is a soul on its own path, with lessons to learn along the way. I do not claim that the channeled perspectives in this book apply to all individuals within a species, or all species, or all wild animals, domesticated animals, or companion animals.

2. As "pure" as any channel would like to be, the fact remains that when messages are conveyed through a consciousness, they are also being filtered by that consciousness, to some degree. While I am committed to keeping personal opinion and beliefs out of the picture, as the channel and

transcriber of the messages, I affect them by the choice of language that I "hear," and what my own level of awareness will allow to come through.

3. On certain topics, e.g. growing older, I received contributions from many animal species. On others, I received only a few. Again, this is just what I have gathered thus far, and it is by no means a complete view of animal perspectives.

4. I gathered the animal insights featured in this book from wild and domesticated animals who currently have their basic needs met: some measure of safety, a home, adequate food, and love. Animals who exist in factory farms, testing labs, and other situations of extreme abuse, neglect, and trauma, or who are starving and/or fleeing natural or human-made disasters, have told me that they must focus on survival and the preservation of their spirit beyond their circumstances. Animals in survival mode are not represented in this book.

5. Animals come through to me in different ways. The tone and content of their statements in this book vary dramatically based upon "who" is talking, what lessons they are learning through their current form, or what

they can share from the vantage point of their formless consciousness. I have included channelings from and conversations with:

a. individual, named animals in sanctuaries

b. my clients' animal partners (names changed to protect client confidentiality)

c. the consciousness or "oversoul" of a given class (Aves aka all birds), genus (Tiger or Elephant), or species (Cobra or Python)

d. the entire animal kingdom as one, aka all animal consciousness

Therefore, you will see messages labeled as HORSE—meaning I received them from all horse consciousness—and you will also see messages from HORSE (Jono)—meaning that Jono, the individual, was speaking to me.

WHY LISTEN TO ANIMALS IN THE FIRST PLACE?

Good question.

Why should we listen to animals when we have plenty of wonderful human thought leaders to look to? How do non-humans bring something to the table that is uniquely healing and empowering for humans?

The answer begins with the most obvious fact: animals are not part of the human condition. They are not ingrained with human beliefs, programming, and habits of being. By their very natures, they see things differently than we do.

The following are some significant aspects of animal existence that differ greatly from our own and provide an explanation of why animals offer us a distinctive way of perceiving and experiencing life. The first two are clearly observable. The third I gleaned from many animal conversations about time, and the rest have been shared by the animals themselves, quite directly. In marked contrast to humans, animals explain that they:

1. Typically spend their lives without looking in a mirror (so their self-concept has nothing to with their appearance).

2. Are not subject to the influence of institutions and organizations such as governments, schools, religions, the medical and scientific communities, corporations and the media, telling them who they are, what events are taking place and what to believe.

3. Do not measure their lives by the clock or calendar. They are aware of different times of the day within the morning, afternoon, evening, and night, a cycle of the moon, a long time versus a short time, and a lifetime. They are not beholden to the concept of time as we are, so there is no such thing as "running late." They experience memories but live in the present moment and do not dwell on a future as it does not exist. [Note: the closer animals are to the human dynamic, the more they are subject to fear and trauma and must work through the memories that ensue.]

4. Embrace "oneness" because they see and feel the interconnectedness, and the "web of life", "the field", or "the grid" among all living things. They recognize themselves as part of a whole that is bigger than they are.

5. Communicate with each other through "a stream of thought and energy" so, even when physically separated, they can stay connected to each other. They use all five senses in conjunction with their sixth sense aka extrasensory perception. In fact, animals view themselves as energy beings first, acutely attuned to the energy fields of other animals, as well as plants, humans and the Earth itself.

6. Observe themselves and others without judgment or comparison.

7. Do not identify with their bodies but, instead, see them as shells or suits that house their "internal light."

8. Have certainty in knowing, not just believing in, the existence of what they refer to as "Spirit" aka "God," "The All," "The Greater," "The Great Gardener," or "All That Is."

9. Know that death is an illusion and that they will return in another form (but they do not know, in advance, which form holds the lessons they will need to learn). They do not fear or resist the cycle of birth and death.

10. Accept the purpose, rhythm, and challenges of life, instead of trying to control them.

11. Know self-love from birth and see no difference between love of self and love for anything or anyone else because all is connected.

12. Understand that their lives are configured to deliver the lessons their souls require for their growth.

In this current time of deep questioning, while old paradigms are crumbling and new ways of being are just beginning to take root within us, the animals' viewpoint can be especially instrumental. Animals clearly and simply direct our attention to the answers that lie within, remind us of our true connection with all living beings, and reinforce the ways of being that are so necessary for us to turn civilization onto a course of unity, wholeness, health, respect, harmony, peace and love.

HOW TO USE THIS BOOK

While *Animal Messages for an Awakening World* provided a doorway into the many facets of animal consciousness, *Animal Insights For Everyday Living* is specifically dedicated to the vision and understanding of non-human animals that may be of help to us. In response to wonderful reader feedback, this book is designed to provide animal wisdom that is easy to reference and digestible in small bites. Most of the communications here have come through since 2017, but a few of the channelings from the first book are included because, as a horse named Jono puts it so succinctly: "We repeat ourselves because the lessons are simple, but humans must hear them over and over again, like the news, until they retain them. The noisy mind lures them back over and over again." Similarly, you may notice that the animals repeatedly mention certain issues—such as life lessons or the importance of stillness or focusing only on what you want to see and create —because these are fundamental stepping stones to embracing greater growth and awareness.

The channelings in this book are arranged to be read, one at a time —as an insight for the day—so they can be integrated into your consciousness. Some of them can even be used as meditations. They are centered, one per page, for this purpose, allowing you to process one line of content at a time.

Whether you select your message by the topic that interests you, or your intuition guides you to a particular page, I hope you will allow yourself the time to absorb what the animals have to say, and allow it to take hold within you. What they have given so freely is for the purpose of increasing your enjoyment, acceptance, and understanding of this ride called Life.

Blessings,

Sandra

CONNECTING
MORE DEEPLY
WITH ANIMALS

CROW

Connect with Us by Sending Out Your Energy

Begin connecting with us by seeing love energy enter you

through the top of your head

and flowing into all your cells.

Then hold up your hands, feel the energy there,

and send out a loving welcome to all beings through your hands

and heart.

We will know that you are reaching out to us!

We are sending our love and appreciation to all of you who dare

to trust what you cannot see.

GECKO

Animals Are Showing Up for Humans Who Are Open

We here in animal land are gathering around people who

seriously want to bridge the gap between us.

You are 'mind openings.'

Be aware of your intention and notice the presence of wild

animals that surround you.

We will never forsake you, and we will keep coming back

until you are ready to pay attention.

You will learn by making time to sit and be open.

Stop looking for conversation.

We will show you humans who we really are if you are simply

open, pay attention, and believe.

GECKO

Allow Connection through Love
Instead of Over-trying

Just sit outside and breathe.

Stare at me. Or another animal. Or a tree.

You don't need fancy exercises.

Release all need.

If you try to connect, you constrict energy flow.

Some of you always try too hard.

Focus on allowing our energy to flow through you.

If you can picture the love coursing within you,

you will be able to feel ours.

HORSE
(DOE)

On Clearing Yourself to Connect with Us

We horses always step in to help anyone trying to move into love.

Your efforts will increase exponentially as a result,

because we are assisting you with your energy field

and energy centers.

We will energetically match anything you do to clear yourself!

For those who want to connect with us,

the most important thing is to first empty your energy garbage

can so you can achieve stillness.

We feel your every emotion, even the tiniest bit

of worry or anxiety.

You humans are carrying around so much now.

Some of you even gather others' energies in bunches

and store them within you.

If it hurts – bury it in the ground.

Some things you may yawn out.

You may even feel sick to your stomach and gag.

Continued...

Your eyes may burn, your throat may feel tight,

and your heart may ache as it lets go of painful rocks.

This is clearing. Good, good, good…let it all go.

You may need some time for this; be patient with yourself.

You get so used to living in a tense state

that you don't realize you're in it.

Peace lies beneath the rubble of human trauma.

LION

Understand Us by Being More like Us

To be more like us:

Feel More.

Do Less.

Stand Back.

Observe.

Absorb.

RABBIT

Believe in Yourself and Release Expectation

If you believe that others can do what you can't,

it will paralyze you every time.

Comparison, jealousy, envy, lack, and putting others 'above you'

are low vibrational thoughts.

To receive from us you must raise your vibration

out of the illusion you have been believing.

Just sitting long enough so the tightness inside relaxes

and the calm feeling arrives

can be enough to get you to where you need to be.

Stillness with no expectation.

All magic comes from this space.

SNAIL

Be Aware of Signs That Messages Await You

The number three is significant.

When you see three of any wild animal species appear undeniably

in your path or in your space,

it is a sign that there is a message waiting for you.

Please don't forget to notice the smallest of creatures.

They may be the ones that facilitate

the greatest understanding within you.

The consciousness of a flea is no less than that of a horse, a whale,

or a human.

SQUIRREL

Come Outside to Tune In

Spend time outside to learn the language of tuning in.

Even if you can't see and hear us,

you must try to come outside every day.

Share the energy out here with us. It helps humans—

and softens you.

For many of you, it will be helpful to write down what you feel

when you're out here.

You can look back, see patterns emerge,

and know you were communicating with us.

Notice the changing feelings in your bodies

when you're outside, too.

The more you pay attention, the more you will feel.

This is how you learn the language

of tuning into yourselves and us.

SQUIRREL

You Must Throw Doubt to the Curb

Those of you who want to commune with us

must believe everything

that you see, feel, hear, sense, and know when we are there.

Otherwise, you create distance between yourselves and us.

Your belief and faith in yourselves are critical.

Stop creating your own self-limitation.

Spend more time letting the information flow through you.

TIGER

Your Contribution is Unique

There can be no comparison between paths and abilities.

Some may show the way,

but the purpose is for all to participate in the return

to wholeness and reconnection.

You are all exquisitely capable.

Each set of gifts—and each journey—is unique

to you and only you.

Every one of you is needed and healing expands

when you share your gifts with others.

You are each filling in different pieces of the puzzle

and seeking to reclaim what has been buried and suppressed

in humans, by humans.

Our strength is your strength.

We await your energetic arrival.

FEAR: WHAT IF, NOT WHAT IS

BAT

Self-Isolation Creates Fear and Anxiety

We animals in the wild do not stow ourselves away

from each other and without resources.

So many human mental issues occur because of this.

Around and around you go in your own heads

with a dark thought or idea,

spinning ever larger like a stick of cotton candy.

All you have to do, instead, is to shift focus onto someone else

or talk it out.

CAMEL

Is Fear of Material Loss
Crippling Your Freedom?

Humans become so tied to what they believe they need

that they fear loss, obsessively.

Follow our lead—discard the trappings that weigh you down.

All those *things* absorb your time, attention, and resources.

Clarity will come when you lighten your load

and let your heart guide your way.

What you believe you cannot live without distances you

from others, your soul's path, and your true Self.

GIRAFFE

Fear Is a Weapon of the Imagination

The human mind creates fear and usually does not know

what a dangerous weapon it has built.

Fear creates the perception of something when nothing is there,

and can keep something present and alive

long after it has disappeared or expired.

Ask yourself, are you afraid of something real

or something your fear imagined?

GIRAFFE

On Mass Fear and Retaining
Your Personal Power

Do not blindly succumb to mass hysteria

by swallowing what you receive through the information media.

These messages are constructed—they are not real.

Losing touch with reality erases all your personal power.

This does not happen in the animal world.

We never lose sight of who we are because

someone is telling us something based in fear.

We ask that you do not allow yourselves to become erased by fear.

Pull away from human messaging that does not arise within you;

Its constant repetition is what gives unreal messages

so much energy and a false 'bigness.'

Do not allow yourselves to lose your sovereignty and

your own inner guidance.

HORSE
(Reese)

Your Fear Blocks Better Outcomes

Humans should not make snap judgments out of fear.

They need to take the time to see how things unfold.

Nothing is what it seems to be.

People give up and walk away before they see the whole picture

or allow things to change more to their liking.

HORSE
(REESE)
How Hurt Becomes Fear

Once humans get hurt—any kind of hurt—

they carry the pain like a chain around their necks

and pull it tight to hold themselves back in fear.

They give up the desire to try.

They grow hard and turn into what they fear most

when they see it in others.

All things mend and heal, even your heart.

Never say 'never again;' it makes you old too fast.

Never give up the desire to try.

LION

Fear Is a Choice: What Do You Choose Now?
(at the time of the Coronavirus)

Fear is the most lethal poison in the well of human existence.

It makes you prey on each other and this goes against natural law.

It weakens your body so it cannot fight

what it would normally overcome.

In the animal kingdom, fear plays a very different role.

It is linked with imminent threats to survival.

You have the choice—right here, right now—to rise above

your historical responses to collective breakdowns

like the one you are facing now.

Declare war on fear because that is the illness

that will destroy you—not a virus.

GRATITUDE
(and What You Might Be
Taking for Granted)

ANACONDA

Appreciate the Benefits of Being Human

Appreciate the flexibility of being human:

to come and go easily and move through the world,

relating to each other without creating fear.

I do not have the choices that humans do.

Your form is not terrifying like mine, so you should be soft

and kind to each other.

Extend yourselves a bit so others feel safe in your presence.

It doesn't take much, a smile or a soft touch.

I cannot do these things, but you can, so, please,

don't miss the opportunity.

BIRDS

Remember We and Your Loved Ones
Are Here

In the morning, stop.

You who sleep, awaken to all of us.

Hear our song. Embrace it with your body. Feel us in your heart.

You may not have any idea of what we are doing energetically.

Love, wisdom, information, encouragement, celebration of life—

we offer all of it to you and we spread it everywhere,

to all living beings.

You need not know what we're saying, but you must trust

that you are being watched over, always.

We carry messages from humans and non-humans

who have crossed over.

We are a physical manifestation of their constant presence

around you.

We know how hard it is for you to believe in what you cannot see

so we do this, willingly.

Owned by no one, we are here for all.

Look up and know.

BUTTERFLY

There Is a Reason We Appear for You

Many notice us but are unaware of our intention when we appear.

When your minds are heavy, filled with stress and worry

or merely distracted,

we try to pull you into a moment of beauty.

If you allow it, we prompt you to use your eyes

instead of your brain,

and to remember all the exquisite beauty that still exists here.

We are not asking you to forget your troubles.

We are asking you to meet us in a moment of delight.

Every animal knows to do this.

Stop and see the butterflies.

PORCUPINE

Don't Overlook the Power of Human Touch
(during the time of Coronavirus-induced
social distancing)

Ahh…so you see a bit through my eyes now,

as you can no longer touch each other freely.

This, too, has happened so you will value the power of love

expressed through human touch.

When your trial of isolation is over,

you can choose to be more loving and use your touch

to express care and concern for others.

This is another opportunity for you to stop taking anything

for granted.

GROWING OLDER, GROWING WISER:

A Different Way of Seeing and Being

ALLIGATOR

Toss the Rushing and Enjoy Being

You wouldn't think I'd have a contribution to make here

but, indeed I do!

When you are in your latter years—like the second half

of your life—flip the proportion.

Spend less time slogging through mud, including emotional mud,

and more time basking in the glow of 'isness.'

Yes, all animals know what that is, and you should too.

If you have spent most of your life striving,

now is the time to allow yourself to just be.

Nature intended for it to be this way.

Catch yourselves when you are driving too fast,

giving in to the habit of rushing.

Do you see me do that?

Heck no – unless there is a tasty dinner morsel awaiting me.

I waddle with a purpose.

Take some notes and try it too.

ANTELOPE

View Your Circumstances without Judgment

We understand that in our current form

we are learning many lessons:

flexibility, consistent cooperation, non-identification

with space, time, or place,

and the diminishment of ego.

You humans would benefit from looking at your circumstances

without emotion or judgment

in order to observe and understand

what your greatest lessons are.

It will explain a lot for every one of you.

CHIMPANZEE

Re-prioritize What's Truly Important

If you have learned life's lessons well,

you will be more content with what is.

Wisdom means not fretting about little things.

It means letting go, focusing on happiness first.

Togetherness. Peaceful interactions.

Gratefulness for all things big and little.

You realize it is a gift to be alive.

I used to get worked up a lot. I don't anymore.

I shrug and don't question so much.

It's all in the plan.

You humans would have a much easier time if you did the same.

COBRA

Speak Your Truth

Aging you say?

If you have learned anything, it is to speak your own truth.

Hiding behind veils for approval—or to hide shame—

colors the decades of your youth.

Now, taste the freedom of your own authenticity.

Lay bare your face, your vulnerability, your needs.

Yes, you all have needs, so stop the pretense

that you've moved beyond them or let them go.

Own them. Own all of your multi-colored self.

CROW

Keep Your Focus on Learning and Enjoying

Our timeline is shorter than yours,

so we have much to learn very quickly.

It all happens faster, and we need to pay attention to our lessons.

This is true for most of the animal kingdom.

Each day marks a new milestone in our awareness.

For humans, we can only say—you would grow faster

and experience much more happiness

if you focused on learning and enjoyment.

The worry, regret, fear, resentment (and worse)

steal the gold from your pots.

Even if you could fly, you would clip your own wings,

as holding grudges and self-punishment are quicksand.

Just remember: Learn, enjoy. Learn, enjoy.

Forgive yourselves and others.

Soar baby—that's what your latter years are for.

DEER

See Yourself as Graceful, Not Brittle

Delicacy is considered a problem by too many young people.

We are gentle, graceful, keenly sensitive,

and observant throughout our lives.

These assets are enhanced with age,

yet humans perceive them as detrimental!

Do not view these qualities as creators of brittleness within you.

Take more care to move through space with ease

and understanding, elegance and grace.

Lightness and fluidity are qualities you possess—

see them in a positive way and they will be so.

Develop a new relationship with space and quiet.

It takes some practice.

You will allow much more beauty into your lives this way,

especially if you see yourselves as part of it.

ELEPHANT

Wisdom Is the Greatest Achievement

Wisdom is not conferred lightly.

It is the goal of a life well-lived and it deserves more respect

in the 'developed' part of human society.

Throughout your life's stages, there are many tasks to complete

that are steppingstones to wisdom.

Physical challenges. Emotional trials. Mental tribulations.

You are assigned those you can handle when you are capable

of doing so, even if it seems otherwise.

You have been climbing ever higher, yet you perceive yourselves

as moving in the opposite direction!

Your perspective is what needs to change.

Instead of 'aging,' see 'accomplishment' or 'advancement.'

ELEPHANT

Physical Form Is Irrelevant to
The Growth of Your Soul

Physical form is irrelevant to the growth of your soul.

Hold onto this concept.

Declare it to yourself as a fundamental truth every day.

You are missing the radiance within you that we see ever growing,

reaching its peak only through time.

Your job is to treasure it.

Walk with your head held high in this knowing —as we do.

GIRAFFE

Your Self Concept Determines How You Age

For us, what you call 'growing older' is just 'growing.'

You think because your skin wrinkles and grows spots

that you have lost beauty,

but you are looking at yourselves through a warped lens.

Remember the eyes and see how they change with time.

The softness and understanding that grow in them

are what you should strive for.

These are eternal gifts.

Beauty is created from within.

Those who see themselves with compassion and admiration

glow from the inside.

Those who rest in negativity and lack self-love

and self-appreciation wither.

You are all roses.

Your blooming and beauty are self-determined.

GOAT

Peace is Your True Power

In youth, you huffed and puffed.

Now, train your breath to be even and smooth.

Power doesn't come from how big a noise you can make.

When you stop the illusion of control

and surrender to God's plan,

you grow in power and beauty.

Acceptance gives you peace.

Peace is power.

GOAT

Reinforce Your Own Light
Through Connection with Others

When you value what you have developed within,

the rest of the world will value it too.

Never see yourself as no longer useful.

Never isolate, as isolation hastens an early death.

Reinforce the power of your own light

by extending yourself to others.

Create community as it once was.

Show the young ones how it's done—growing older

doesn't kill your spirit.

Your spirit simply grows bigger

and takes up more space in your shell.

GORILLA

Choose Your Beliefs and Your Body Will Follow

The illnesses that you associate with aging

are illnesses of the mind.

We cannot impress this upon you enough.

Thoughts of self-limitation and being too old

are toxic and crippling.

We never think this way.

You have the power to change the reality of your body,

but pills, supplements, and fancy programs

will not do this for you.

Instead, flip your perspective, and do it every day.

Those who are vital, clear of mind, and flexible of body,

have chosen their beliefs.

The brain and body then follow suit.

GORILLA

The Secret to Rekindling Your Own Flame

Go back to focusing on what you can bring to the world,

and what beauty you can see within yourself and others.

By reorienting yourself to the sweet magic

of what really matters in life,

your inner flame will be forever rekindled.

GORILLA

Fill Your Time with What Fuels Your Soul

Laziness and repetition will age you.

Remember this when you choose the activities

that fill your time—are they feeding your soul?

The more you give your soul the fuel to direct your life,

the more you will be renewed.

HIPPO

Stay Young by Remembering
What You Knew As a Child

There is, indeed, a secret to shining through your latter years.

It's all about the vibes and I know more and more of you

are catchin' my drift.

Success means being young in attitude and reclaiming

what you knew as children.

Leave the strive and drive behind.

Return to the sweetness of giving and receiving.

HIPPO

Up Your Fun to Slow Your Aging

The grandmas and grandpas who are the most fun

have slowed down their aging.

Start dancing even if you never have—

even if you think you have two left feet.

Even if you're alone in your house.

Be the moth and gravitate to little ones and non-human folks.

They have very strong light within them

that can brighten your own being.

Lighten up and your soul will be glad.

HORSE
(ALBERT)

Find the Magic beyond the Mundane

Humans are always peering through a hole.

When you have spent enough time in your current form,

you can better see the big picture, if you allow it.

Intention. Synchronicity. Signs.

This living Universe is talking to you

and bringing you gifts all the time.

'Aging' can be your excuse to broaden your view

beyond the mundane.

The young are obsessed with shiny things—pleasing the body,

acquiring, controlling, defining—

stuff they think they need.

All illusion, my friends.

If our lives were only what you see on the outside—

in and out of a box, moving in a circle, and back into the box—

we would go mad.

The inner life is where the magic happens.

HORSE
(KODAK)

Concentrate on Presence and Energy, Not Things

As you become less tied to achieving in the third dimension,

spend more time in the spiritual realms.

Let things fall away; lighten your load of negative emotions.

Dump the bucket, so to speak.

Less identification with form allows you to fly

as your One True Nature.

Spend more time giving out energy, not things.

Presence without distraction is the key in all situations,

and it is quite fulfilling, you will see!

The principles we share with you don't change,

but your willingness and ability to live them

can increase as you move through time.

PANDA

Take a Gentler Approach

We live a long time and we know how things change

inside bodies.

Make your movements softer and gentler

and let your thoughts go along for the ride.

Do your best to discard anything stressful,

as its impact is harder on you as you age.

PANDA

Pause and Laugh at Yourself

Watch and listen more—you'll notice details you missed

when you were younger.

There is magic in the pause (paws...got it?).

Find the funny, especially in yourself.

PANDA

Give Advice Only When Asked

Make the time to commune with others,

especially those younger than you.

You will feel good if they ask for your guidance and wisdom.

Always wait to be asked first.

No one likes a preachy papa or mama.

RABBIT

Your Lessons Create Your Circumstances

Many humans feel that they're not fully living

unless they are with each other.

If you find yourself physically alone,

realize it is an opportunity for you

to reach important understandings.

The lessons you are here to learn create the structure around you.

Circumstances arrange for your highest growth.

RHINO

Stop Stomping and Sway Instead

Growing older is like a dance:

you have to learn new steps,

to music that is different from what you used to listen to.

When young, you stomp—making your mark on the world.

You discover your own strength by kicking up a lot of dust.

Through time, you spend less time trying to make a statement.

You hear more of the universe's melody,

instead of trying to make your own.

If you allow yourselves to grow in awareness,

you sway to God's rhythm.

RHINO

Keep an Open Mind for a Flexible Body

If you don't pay attention and you allow your thinking

to grow rigid,

your body will harden like glue.

Use your mind now to loosen up your grip on the reins.

Let go of your own expectations.

Let the carriage take you.

ROBIN

This Life Is Just One Adventure in Your Soul's Journey

Growing older does not exist the same way for us as for you.

If you define yourselves only within the limits of 3D reality,

you are a prisoner of time.

If you grasp the immortality of your soul,

you will see that every lifetime is a page in your book,

adding adventures to your story.

The end of this life is just a page turning,

sometimes giving way to an entirely new chapter.

The only difference is that you will not remember

most of the previous pages.

Make no mistake though, you are constantly progressing.

Every life brings you to a new place,

and the story of your soul's journey grows richer.

SHEEP

Take Bigger Risks to Express Your True Self

Growing older means taking bigger risks,

but they are different from the gambles of youth.

Dare to be you in ways you never have been before.

You don't have to jump out of an airplane.

(Although you could do that if you like; I just fail to see

why you would want to.)

Whereas you felt you had something to prove to yourself

or others in your earlier years,

now you can truly live from the inside out.

Send a big hello to strangers.

Try something just out of curiosity.

Who cares about the outcome?

ZEBRA

Every Life Path Is Important
and Equally Valuable

Perhaps it will help if you see as we do.

We view everything as steps leading upward.

We may wobble, but we are forever progressing

toward our destination.

Our whole life purpose may simply be to run together in a herd,

and not step on anyone else's hooves.

We might show up in this life to sharpen our intellect,

to understand how things fit together,

or to learn how to get along with others harmoniously.

Our path, in this form, may even be to more fully know God,

because we had been human and could never feel

our connection and importance.

All of these challenges are equally valuable.

You can never compare anyone's experiences with others.

We also know, with every inch of our being,

that we are here only until we learn our most important lesson.

The ones we don't learn, we will work on in another lifetime.

HEALTH AND HEALING:
ANIMAL STRATEGIES
TO HELP YOU THRIVE

DOG
(MISTER T)

Free Healing That's Available to Everyone

Set aside time to be outside.

Put it on a calendar, like a doctor's appointment.

You wouldn't miss that, would you?

Well, this healing may be even more important,

but no one talks about it,

because it is free to all and not advertised on TV.

DOG
(MISTER T)

Help Your Heart in All That You Do

The task for humans is to realize and maintain the fullness of love

in their hearts.

This requires attention to the quiet, little thoughts,

not those 'big statements' you use to manifest results.

If a person gives one hundred percent of their attention

to what they are doing at the moment,

they remove the worrisome little noises that hurt the heart.

DOG
(MISTER T)

Healthy Habits as Important
as Eating Vegetables

If you eat, just eat, and pay attention to each bite.

When you are in conversation, pay total attention

to the other person.

When you write, only write,

and when you walk, concentrate your awareness

on your surroundings, taking everything in.

These are my recommendations for staying healthy—

every bit as important as eating your vegetables.

Maybe even more so.

ELEPHANT
(MATRIARCH)
On Handling a Healing Crisis

Ah, the human healing crisis.

We do not use any other words to describe the times

when you are physically and emotionally challenged.

We experience them as well, but not as severely as humans

because we expect them,

we do not fear them,

and we always envision ourselves beyond them.

This is how you can best navigate them, as we do:

1. Keep your life as normal as possible.

2. Add more things that make you laugh.

3. Meditate and visualize yourself every day as already fully healed.

4. Do not talk about your issues—your cells are listening and they will assume the form you speak about.

5. Plan all the activities you can still do—write them down in a list and put them into your schedule.

Continued...

6. Spend time with your friends and loved ones; focusing on being with them gets you out of your head. We never walk alone.

7. Do not question the 'why.' Sometimes these trials are actually protective and you will not understand how until further down the road. The Creator's wisdom stretches far beyond what we can see.

GECKO

Release Constriction and
Resistance to Prevent Dis-ease

The density of form is perceived; it is just an illusion.

It's a value you assign to your situation, but it is made up!

Everything is fluid—including you.

Start seeing this with your mind.

Even what you call cancer is just energy that has not been allowed

to move appropriately.

Yes, I know about cancer and all such things. We all do.

Visualize all constrictions and resistance

moving out of you every day.

This cleanses you of what becomes dis-ease.

HIPPO

Joy Is the Overlooked Piece to a Healthy Life

I mention quite often that the missing piece in human life is joy.

It is also your ticket to 'healthy.'

You must stop the addiction to being serious,

if you want to heal or remain healthy.

HORSE

Address the Energy Field in Order to Heal

All the healing we do on humans and on each other

is done on the energetic level,

because energy is what every single being is made of.

We address the different layers of what you call the aura;

we also clear the energy centers of your body.

We release constricted energy, dissolve energy blocks,

and replace them with lots of high-frequency energy (love).

Humans do themselves a terrible disservice

by ignoring their energy field when healing.

They do not know it can fracture or suffer from holes,

if the human body is invaded by injury or procedures.

Then they wonder why—long after an operation—

they have not fully healed.

It will benefit humans to learn how to clear their own fields,

or work with a good energy healer

to assist on the pathway of healing.

KANGAROO
(WILLIAM)

On Loving Yourself to Health

People who heal, and rise beyond their own expectations

and circumstances,

have learned that loving themselves above all is the key.

The more you love yourself, the more you heal

physically and emotionally.

LION

Turn First to Nature for Healing

The human physical body has a slow, dense resonance,

making you believe you need very strong medicine.

But most of you do not try healing with Nature first,

before running to human-made preparations

that can have ill effects.

We suggest you consider what we do.

We know to stop eating to release poisons from the body.

We understand the importance of pure water,

and find another source if ours becomes unclean.

We use the power of sunshine and sleep

to bring us back to balance.

And we put our paws upon the Earth

to receive her healing energy.

Some humans know about healing plants,

which are very powerful,

but they need to stick to natural amounts

and not over-concentrate.

Nature already knows the best proportions for healing.

Continued...

There are also cycles of the moon

that are most auspicious for healing,

and we make sure to connect with the moon's energy then.

Most of all, if humans understood the importance of patience

in the healing process,

they wouldn't force their bodies so hard, which can backfire.

You must see the lesson in the healing journey, as we do.

OSTRICH

Be Flexible with Your Attitude and
Time in Order to Heal

Flexibility is of utmost importance for recovery,

especially in two areas: attitude and time.

Attitude—the more inflexible your thinking,

the more you slow your healing.

Regardless of what anyone tells you,

you must see your body as a regenerative energy machine,

always creating the new.

Time—be fluid with your time and devote more of it

to the care of both your mind and body.

Stillness and laughter are central to the healing process.

Time in Nature, you already know, is medicine in itself,

but you must make space for it apart from

any health treatments you might be receiving.

These may seem obvious but are especially important

for those of you who are still up and about

and keep pushing yourselves too hard.

You must let your body take the lead

or you will keep going backwards.

RATTLESNAKE

Direct Your Thoughts to Create Health

Do not give in to the insidious fear about health in your society.

The medical community is held captive

by those who make money from your fear,

with expensive testing, drugs, and more.

Furthermore, they still know little about the cause of disease.

You take on fear when a doctor examines you,

and then you question your own health,

instead of directing your thoughts to create health.

Letting go of blocked energy—including in the mind—is the key.

SHEEP

Let Your Love Out Daily to Stay Healthy

Let that big, beautiful heart of yours out of its cage.

Failure to let the love out causes heart trouble.

Find ways to show your love to any being—

human (including yourself), animal, or plant.

Send love to anyone, every single day.

HELPING ANIMALS
AND THE PLANET

ALL ANIMALS
To Create the New, Stop Focusing on All That Is 'Wrong'

Stop concentrating on everything that is wrong

and things that cause your hearts pain.

A new paradigm cannot be built on an old foundation

that is crumbling.

To build a strong structure and create positive change,

operate only from an elevated place.

You cannot do this when you are in a state of reaction,

because you are matching your energy to what you don't want

to see, experience, or create.

ALL ANIMALS

Put Your Energy into What You All Share

Go back to the basics.

Water. Soil. Air.

Every single being needs these three things to be healthy.

The basics will reunite you so that your focus is not on opinion,

which divides you.

Focus only on your common needs and concerns.

ALL ANIMALS

Take These Actions to Heal Nature

To heal Nature, three kinds of effort are needed.

The first two are done through focused meditation
and energy work.

First, focus on clearing constricted energy in the form of
pollution, beliefs, wounds, and scars.

Second, raise the frequency of the space you want to heal
to the vibration of love.

The third step is to take action and participate in the healing
in a way that matters to you.

Anything you do that helps and heals
ultimately benefits everyone.

ALL ANIMALS
Guidance for Those Who Want to Volunteer

Pick one cause and let the effort spread like wildfire.

Do not overburden yourselves and do not go it alone.

Ask friends to join you in an endeavor.

Most importantly, do only what allows you to remain happy

and not stressed.

Participation is important because the vibration rises

and multiplies when people come together.

You can also keep each other buoyant during challenging times.

You have all been disempowered through your beliefs.

By coming together to rectify what is out of balance,

you will reclaim your power.

CAT
(LEAH)

The Power of Your Intention Creates Change

The growing number of you who see with your hearts

is the reason animals have hope for humanity and Earth.

It is incumbent upon you to know the value and power

of your intentions to create good in the world.

This does not mean you have to volunteer;

it means choosing kind and loving thoughts and actions

every day.

CRAB

Your Love and a Little Care Go a Long Way

The sea and all of us in it are suffering,

but love will prevail. Yes, love will win,

if you realize that no moments can be spent feeding darkness

with your intention and energy.

When you visit the oceans, treat them with respect and reverence

as we do.

Know that you are surrounded with love from

beings like me.

If you enter the oceans with your hearts open, we will feel it.

Join us in the celebration of goodness—

which is the only real truth.

Stop looking at the size of the problem.

A little care goes a long way.

ELEPHANT

Create a Ripple Effect with Every Small Act

Create a ripple effect and partner with us in the awakening.

Every single act that spreads awareness, health,

regeneration, and love

goes into the Web [of Life].

We—and all animals—feel it,

even if humans do not.

Spread the ways of collaboration that honor the Earth Mother.

HIPPO

Why Giving Back Must Be Joyful

Even when you contribute your time and energy

to make the world a better place,

if you never laugh—if you are not enjoying it—

switch to something else.

Otherwise, you are lowering the vibration

(yours and the planet's)

and you are stressing your health.

HORSE
(DALTON)
How You Can Partner with Us Now to Help All

Set aside time every evening for this visualization:

Imagine you are sending light to illuminate minds

and that it will continue throughout the night.

Picture the unsticking of those who are bound by old ideology

and habitual ways of thinking.

Next, see the hardness around people's hearts, borne of fear,

dissolving easily,

with only love remaining.

Finally, envision all people feeling love for themselves,

forgiving themselves,

and going out into the world choosing their actions,

and making all choices,

from a place of inner security, peace, and compassion.

This is how you can partner with us to help all.

HORSE
(HONEY BEE)
On Helping the Earth with Your Love

Send blessings and love out to Gaia each day.

Thank her for her beauty and gifts.

Plant flowers and trees so you keep populating the Earth

with beautiful life.

Pick up trash, hug a tree, and listen to the wind

with reverence and appreciation.

Your love will help Nature flourish more than you know.

HORSE
(JENNIE MARIE)

How You Can Help Horses

Change the way we are seen.

Bring softness and love into every interaction.

Watch us intently and closely; we will show you so much

with small movements.

Honor our differences.

Believe in what you cannot see—

that we are all connected,

that we know your thoughts,

and that we receive information in many different ways.

Every night, visualize us all as whole, healed, and loved

across the world.

HORSE
(STORMY)

Some Powerful Steps
That Create Positive Change

Stand up for what you believe in—

but do it by coming from positivity and love.

Stay focused on conscious creation, not minutiae.

See calm waters ahead; paint calm into the picture of your life.

Approach each other with softness and love.

Picture healing happening across the globe and it will.

Let go of tightness and expectation.

Spend more time becoming one with All.

Let stillness permeate you.

This is how to create change.

LION

See Only Solutions for Them to Materialize

Enter and stay in our world,

where energy, consciousness, and connection take center stage.

You humans will never understand this

if you watch us from the outside.

You must feel us in your hearts.

If you want to help us, use your mind's eye

to see our populations thriving, our Earth healing,

and compassion and regeneration reigning.

Just as we do, send love and energy

into the planet you walk upon.

You cannot come up with solutions

if you rest in the old ways of being.

MOUSE

Replace Ignorance with Kindness

Notice that the root of ignorance is 'ignore.'

This is the lesson at play now across humanity—

you can no longer close your eyes to how you live,

entertain yourselves, and use other beings

—human and non-human—

as well as Mother Earth and her resources.

Do not give into blame of self, others,

or even corporations and governments.

Consider the how and why of your actions.

What are you supporting and where are you putting your energy

(aka money)?

Are you sure that you really want that thing to grow?

If kindness is at the root of your decisions,

you understand what we are saying.

TIGER

What Lies Within, Shows Up All around You

Stop clinging to the notion of how bad things are.

Instead, celebrate the good that has already been created.

Much more kind-heartedness is at play in the world

than you know, because it is not publicized to the masses.

The rest of the work is all internal,

but most humans still do not understand the connections

between what you think, how you feel,

and what occurs outside of you.

As within, so without.

TIGER

Choose The Imprint You Want to Leave Behind Each Day

Spend your time carving new pathways

for gratitude, love, joy, wonder,

softness, and generosity to flow within you.

You will feel so much better when you deliberately choose

what you want to leave behind you

as you move through your day.

Just watch what unfolds and know that it is all felt

in the Web [of Life],

forever and for always, affecting the collective,

even if you cannot see the visible results.

All exists in energy first, then materializes into form.

INCREASING YOUR HAPPINESS, POSITIVITY, AND JOY

THE ANIMALS' WAY

DOLPHIN

Joy Results When You Stop Thinking

You feel joy when you give yourself a mental break

and absorb the magic of the moment.

Sometimes it takes days, weeks, months, or years to get to joy,

and it may only last a moment.

However, with practice, you start stringing together

more and more visits to this place.

DOLPHIN

Joy Requires No One Else but You

You may be alone or with another person when you feel joy,

but experiencing your true nature

—not experiencing another person—

is what creates joy.

The other person's love acts as a mirror,

making it easier for you to see yourself.

But it is always you experiencing you

that results in joy.

ELEPHANT

Tell Your Eyes What to See to Stay Positive

Humans do not realize that we—and all animals—

work hard to stay positive.

We are very aware of the human condition

and the resulting state of Mother Earth.

But to keep going and see the good, we know we must look for it.

We decide what we look at.

What is positive gets our attention, not the other stuff.

If you make a consistent effort to attend to the positive,

you will get better at it.

Talk to your eyes; give them direction on what to look for,

and you will indeed see it.

Stay on this level.

Do not get caught up in details that weigh you all down.

The big picture is what will keep you buoyant.

ELEPHANT

Stay Upbeat through Selective Listening

Humans have so many opinions and rules coming at them
all the time.

We suggest that you spend time choosing very carefully

what—and how much of—

other humans' noise you want to listen to.

We believe it should be a very small percentage.

The majority of what you must listen to

is from the highest version of your Self.

You can only hear it in the quiet.

ELEPHANT

Unburden Yourself to Feel More Joy

Discard objects that weigh you down.

Stop obsessing about dirt and perfect cleanliness—it is silly.

Slow down and enjoy the magic of simple things.

Stop focusing on what you cannot change.

ELEPHANT

A Few Suggestions to Remember
What Brings You Joy

We make sure we focus on what brings us joy:

Little ones and their antics.

A good game—some of us like balls to play with.

Mudbaths, and fully registering the experience

with all our senses. (You could say this is our spa.)

And always, the beauty of Mother Earth, her sunrises

and sunsets, clouds and breezes.

These are examples of how we are kind to ourselves.

Perhaps these will remind you humans of what brings you joy,

in case you have forgotten.

ELEPHANT
(MATRIARCH)
Being Lighter Brings You Better Results

We elephants know a lot about joy

and we have wonderful senses of humor.

Humans do not yet grasp that being happy is not just a nice idea.

The most successful outcomes arise from a light approach!

Remember the vibration!

The lighter you are, the more light you create—and attract.

ELEPHANT
(Matriarch)

Giving to Others by Choice Creates Happiness

Humans are happy when they give to others without obligation

or the need to prove their own worth.

Many still do not realize that they are designed this way.

Looking beyond yourselves takes the pressure off for a while!

Elephant
(Matriarch)

The Human Experience Is One of Many

Regard the human condition as part of everything—

not separate, not above.

This way of seeing will help you immensely.

Humans suffer from lack of perspective.

This life is not the only act in the play, so it is impossible to do,

experience, or be everything now.

If you view your current experience as one of many

that your soul will have,

you just might enjoy your life more.

ELEPHANT
(MATRIARCH)

Sweep Out What Is Stressful and What Remains Is Joy

Joy doesn't have to look a certain way.

Some jump up and down. Others are more internal;

their joy is a quiet simmer, not a rolling boil.

Who is anyone to judge?

Sometimes joy is simply the absence of negativity,

if you see it that way.

Sweep out all that is stressful and what remains is joy.

HIPPO

Human Adults Must Remember
to Go Out and Play

Humans need to be reminded to go out and play,

for goodness sake!

Dance and sing and eat and flirt and hug and kiss

and do those human things,

because human is what you are

and there is good that goes with that.

HIPPO

Reapportion Your Time to Include Some Fun

Fun doesn't have to have consequences!

You serious types are putting the kibosh on my strategies.

Fun doesn't slow down your growth—it speeds it up!

Now more than ever, you need to discover your sense of humor!

Stop listening to the 'shoulds' and 'oughtas'—

they shorten your life.

Reapportion your time. It's lopsided.

Balance is the key.

Time in stillness. Time in play. Time in work and 'to-dos.'

HORSE
(HONEY BEE)
De-complicating Things Brings You Joy

Seek joy within and without;

this is the crucial piece missing from your puzzle.

If you cannot find joy in Nature,

find it in the eyes and laugh of another being.

Walk in the water, sing a song, dance, giggle.

These things are good for you and everything around you.

The process of de-complicating things brings joy and healing.

Use your senses—cherish them—for they are gateways to joy.

HORSE
(SWEET LOU)

Fun Happens When You Put Down Your To-do List

We horses know how to have fun.

Fun means not thinking, for a change.

It means not striving to perfect something,

make an impression, learn something,

clean up after yourself, or fix something that is broken.

Fun is simply breathing in beautiful scents from the air,

being able to run, tasting lovely things,

being with someone you care about, even just doing nothing!

I am not sure, but I think people expect fun

to knock their socks off.

No! Fun does not have to shock your adrenaline into overdrive.

The definition of fun, I think, is gratitude for being able

to stop doing your 'to-do' list.

ORANGUTAN

Pause and See the Pretty

Here is how to make your chores feel like play—

whatever you are doing,

pause to see the prettiness in something or someone.

It makes the to-dos go faster.

Stop and look at the butterflies, they are magical creatures.

Little bits of lightness, that is what you need.

The more you do this, the more the bits of prettiness and light

will show up for you.

You become a magnet attracting them to you,

to add sparkle to your day.

PANDA

Do Something Harmless That Makes You Laugh

You need to laugh at least once a day, 'bear minimum.'

Find something harmless that makes you laugh.

Forget being human and just be, instead.

Sit on your bum bun like we do.

Build a sandcastle, play an instrument or cards.

Smile.

LOOKING WITHIN
FOR YOUR GREATEST
ANSWERS

ALL ANIMALS

Approach Meditation in Your Own Unique Way

Reach into the silence. Your true stillness is calling.

Let go of formalities.

Following others' way of doing things puts you in a state

of striving and forcing.

Your meditation can be journaling, channeling, walking—

anything that gives your busy mind a break.

It can be what is longing to come out,

or longing to draw you inward,

if you have been living only in your outer-ness.

You must do this your own way.

Make no mistake—the voice of your inner knowing

is growing louder and louder.

ALL ANIMALS

On Collaborating with Animals in Meditation

We have been waiting for this opportunity

to work together energetically.

Call upon our assistance when you set an intention

to spread healing and love.

You will never get resistance when you request our help

to heal Mother Earth,

and any and all creatures who dwell upon her.

You may imagine one species at a time,

or you may also call upon us as a global collective.

Don't be surprised if you see our faces when you close your eyes

and summon us.

Envision us side by side with you in a circle.

Include this vision in every healing.

It does not matter if you personally cannot feel it

and have no proof.

Know that it is done.

This is the most important collaboration that could ever happen

among our species.

BEAR

Your Stillness Helps More Than Just You

Discovering your inner stillness will do more good for everyone

than you could possibly know.

This is an energetic planet and your own quietude

makes it easier on us all.

When you are still, we do not have to cut through human frenzy.

Oneness works in your favor, because giving yourselves peace

means you give it to us too.

BEAR

On the Healing Effects of Solitude

I speak often of the healing effects of solitude

and the regeneration of body and soul that it affords.

Silence is where your answers lie, where peace and safety dwell.

It is where you are not judged, so why judge yourself

when you are in silence?

You can stop performing like a circus toy.

You can find your own heartbeat and cherish it.

Solitude is your savior.

BLUE JAY

Let the Love In to Fill up Your Cup

There is so much love around you,

but you are not allowing it to enter you.

Come outside and close your eyes.

For a change, stop trying to send energy or love or anything else.

Instead, receive what we are sending you.

Feel the waves of love wash over you.

This is how your fill your own cup

so that you will have more to give.

CAT
(COOKIE)

See from Your Soul, Not Your Personality

We see you humans suffer

because you are locked into your perception.

For example, when something does not happen as you hoped,

you do not see the alternative path.

You block it with your negativity, remorse, and mourning

over the 'failure' of your original plan.

There is always a reason for why things go awry.

You have a bigger path, but you cannot see it through ego eyes.

You need to access your wise eyes and see from your soul.

GECKO

Close Your Eyes to Escape
Your Limited Self-concept

Stop running about from task to task!

Frenetic activity gets in the way of soul growth.

You must be brave to sit still and go within.

Empty your mind. Close your eyes.

This takes you out of the illusion of form

and the limits of your self-concept.

See how everything is right in its pure state?

The stillness you feel is what is really inside you!

You must take time away from buildings and other humans

to find yourselves again and again.

GECKO

A Meditation on Your Own Greatness and Limitlessness

Realizing your own greatness—your own limitlessness—

is a challenge for humans.

You are much bigger than your shell.

You are not your body.

You are not your thoughts.

Close your eyes. Feel your edges melt away and blend with all.

Imagine the vastness of the energy around you.

Allow your hands to connect to it.

Stay with it until you feel it in your chest.

All of this is you and more.

You and your energy are part of the vastness.

There is no boundary and no limit.

In energy we are all one.

You can call upon the energy and power of the All

whenever you wish.

HORSE

Getting Started with Meditation

Having a hard time getting started?

Do you feel like you are on the outside looking in?

Sit down outside if you can.

All you need to do is sit patiently and focus on your heart.

Notice how your heart lets go

and the tightness in your chest relaxes.

Close your eyes. Do you see vibrations, patterns, colors,

or just calm darkness? It is all perfect.

Focus on gratitude—that you are surrounded

by peace, energy, and love.

Listen to the symphony of sounds in your ears.

Feel the air on your skin.

Resist the urge to leave.

Fight the urge to do something.

Your patience paves the way for insight to unfold.

HORSE
(WOODROW)

When You Meditate with Horses, Your Awareness Blooms

We horses are here to help those who are trying

to move humans and the planet forward.

You see, you need energetic knives to cut through the illusion

of the human world around you.

Horses are sensitive enough to see what is going on for you,

and compassionate enough to help.

Not all species are the same—

you learn different things from each.

More and more humans need to share the power

of meditating with horses!

If you separate yourself from daily life and sit near us in the quiet,

you will experience profound change.

In our presence, awareness blooms.

You will start to hear, see, feel, and know the truth

that lies beyond the prison of the mind.

SHEEP

The Seat of Creation is Stillness

Silence and stillness are not nothingness.

They are where all creation begins.

Embrace silence.

Embrace stillness.

LOVE:
EXPANDING YOUR
APPRECIATION
OF WHAT YOU ARE

ALL ANIMALS

Love Already Binds You to Everything and Everyone

Love is the living fabric that connects all living things.

It holds together the threads that make up the Web of Life.

So, you see: You are already bound to each other by love,

even if you don't know it.

ALL ANIMALS

A Practice to See through the Eyes of Love, as We Do

To experience and expand the love within you,

as you go about your daily life,

imagine you are flipping a switch behind your eyes

that turns on a pink light bulb.

Now you can look softly upon what you see

and truly notice all that is beautiful about it.

You will notice a calming effect spreading through you.

You may even find your mouth upturned in a quiet smile;

this is because you have raised your vibration

and you are seeing through the eyes of love, as we do.

BEAVER

A Trick for Tapping into The Love inside You

Look tenderly upon one being you love—

your pet, your beloved, your child.

Hold that feeling inside you like a beautiful, colored ball of light.

Make it your favorite color.

Mentally send that ball of light to each person you encounter—

even online!

Energy and intention know no boundaries.

Make it your mission to share the gift of your light

with as many people as possible.

This practice will return you to your purpose once again,

like a computer reboot!

CROW

On Loving Your Way through Negative Emotions

When you start getting upset, no matter the reason,

stop what you are doing and put it down.

Go to another room. Or step outside. Just breathe.

Tap into the love in your heart.

Do not let the snowball start to skid downhill.

This way, you won't have to regret your tone

or any negative energy you might put out.

Observing yourself in the middle of acting out

is the first step to positive change within.

DOG
(MISTER T)

On How to Let Love Be Your Purpose

I hear people asking about their 'purpose.'

Love is the purpose.

Stop whatever it is you're doing and love more.

You do not have to worry what your next step will be—

love will take you there.

Keep talking to the love in your heart.

The answers are not outside of you.

They are not in your brain, either.

Ask: 'Where will love take me today?

Where can I express it most, to whom or what?'

It may surprise you where you go when you ask this question,

but no traditional path will take you where your soul needs to be.

DOG
(MISTER T)

On How to Evolve in Love

Start small, where it feels easiest to love—

with people who welcome it.

You can, with time, move on to giving love to those who reject it,

because they are covered by emotional wounds and scars.

Work your way up the scale to ever more challenging situations.

This is how you evolve in love.

DOG
(MISTER T)

Real Love Is Presence,
Not Distraction from Your Self

Many of you do not appreciate the love you have

and it makes me sad.

What are your expectations?

Why does it seem they cannot be realized?

Look at the ones in your life who love you.

All that matters is love—any love.

Why do so many of you feel incomplete

without a specific kind of love?

You are missing the point—real love is presence,

not distraction to run away from yourself.

HORSE
(Caspian)
On Being Love

Love is not something people understand.

They think it is a pretty picture like in a movie,

something to be received.

They have it backwards.

Love is something that comes from inside you

because it is what you're made of.

Just let it out.

The universe gives back to you what you send out,

so the love will always flow back to you.

HORSE
(HUGO)

On Raising Your Vibration to Love

To activate the love within you,

put your hand on your heart before you start your day.

Vibrationally, you will shift into the good.

We, the animals, are here to help you.

Envision yourself proceeding through your day

with peace and love filling your heart.

Feel the waves of love wash over you

and see them emanating from you.

All of you can access this at any time.

KANGAROO
(WILLIAM)

Self-Love Means Looking
behind Another's Words

Few understand what self-love really means or how far it extends.

It means not believing the wobbly feeling in your gut

when someone criticizes you.

When someone points out, kindly or otherwise,

what you might consider doing better,

self-love means taking time to digest what they are saying

and asking yourself if it is really true.

Remember: their agendas, broken parts, and egos talk, too.

KANGAROO
(WILLIAM)

Self-Love Is Noticing the Delusions of Your Mind

Self-love means noticing where your own mind goes,

because it can tell you lies about who you are—

lies that cripple you with pain, label you, and pigeonhole you.

This may be the root of all suffering

and the hardest lesson to learn.

Self-love means knowing your essential worth

without needing proof, and based on no result at all.

SHEEP

Self-Love is Knowing You Are You for a Reason

Self-love is knowing that if you were supposed to be an angel,

you would be,

and that if you showed up in the world as the person you are,

it is for a reason.

I hope this will give you some degree of comfort—

nothing is an accident, least of all you.

SHEEP

Loving Yourself Means Not Selling Out

If you love yourself,

you get the vote of confidence that you can succeed

in the face of any challenge,

and you do not give in to self-doubt.

It is knowing that being true to yourself is the priority,

and that you will not sell out for any amount,

any lifestyle,

anything,

or anyone.

SHEEP

Self-Love Means Being Patient

Self-love means not only being patient with yourself,

but also with the universe and its timeframe

for delivering the best scenarios for your growth and happiness.

It is remembering that you are worth the wait!

WOLF

On Experiencing Divine Love

There is treasure buried within you.

It is the presence of divine love that you will find there—

your true nature.

You cannot access this when you are in the company of another.

You can access human love and compassion then,

but divine love is a one-on-one experience.

It is felt and understood only in stillness.

MANIFESTATION:
Creating Your Experience
From Behind Your Eyes

ALL ANIMALS

Your External World Must
Be Changed from the Inside

It is not a new concept that you will change events and outcomes

by changing your inner focus.

But given the state of your current 3D world,

perhaps enough of you will see that the only truths you will find

—and the only place where you will be empowered

as an individual— is in the court of your Self.

The best thing to do is concentrate

on your thoughts and emotions.

By choosing the ones that feel good,

you don't just benefit your own health,

you also raise the vibration of other people, animals, plants,

and anything and everything you can imagine.

From a higher vibrational state, better policies will be created.

You are not small.

Most of you are not being run by your governments,

your military, or your religions.

You absolutely must understand that, especially in numbers,

you will change your world from the inside.

GECKO

On Disciplining the Human Mind

We know most of you are better than you think you are.

Why do so many of you dislike yourselves so much?

We believe it is because your minds say things

that you are ashamed of

and you beat yourselves up for it.

Your mind is just a wild noisemaker.

Yes, you use the mind to create and accomplish things,

but you don't discipline it!

Keep the good stuff it produces and spit out the rest.

The good stuff is what makes you and others feel good

and whole and peaceful.

Directing your mind is the challenge of being human.

We—all animals—hear your thoughts, so we know.

ELEPHANT

You Can Shape Reality with
the Energy of Thought

Just the way you can believe in God, angels, guides, or Spirit,

also believe that everything is energy

—including your thoughts and intentions—

and these shape reality.

This is something you all can do: Sit.

Hold the vision of a world that works.

Lead with your hearts as you care for all beings and things.

Now you are reshaping reality.

Trust in this—see it spread worldwide—

joining all in the celebration of Oneness.

HARE

Use Courage and Discipline
to Bring Forth Abundance

Abundance is our birthright, yours and ours.

To help us and the Earth Mother,

have the courage and the discipline to manifest your reality

every day.

See it behind your eyes.

Manifest peace, joy, abundance, honesty, brotherhood, and love—

it is all there.

HARE

Generosity and Trust Attract
Help from the Universe

When your vision is to give, you gain the aid of the universe,

and you manifest results even faster.

Giving includes giving to self!

Once you turn your efforts over to trust,

you raise your vibration so the universe steps up to meet you.

It is a reward for lessons well learned.

HORSE

Soften Your Lens to Expand
What You Want to See

Practice focusing on the softness behind your eyes.

See the world through a lens of gentleness, beauty,

kindness, and safety.

When you soften what you see, you are creating as you do.

You may call it a child's imagination,

but it is actually sophisticated manifestation that anyone can do.

HORSE
(Emilion)

Forget Some of the Things You've Been Taught

You humans are all raised backwards.

Every. Single. One of you.

You are trained to await every next obstacle,

as if you will be better prepared and your road will be easier.

The anticipation then paralyzes you

so you cannot even take the next step.

You are actually being taught to create—

and then cope with—misery!

Instead, you must direct your mind

to build the happiness you want.

Every species will tell you that you humans are all creating

exactly what you see and experience.

You must all begin to feel and listen to your hearts,

or you will keep creating more of what you already see.

LION

Your Thinking Must Be Your First Priority

Humans are addicted to overthinking and dredging up the past

like an old bone, to foretell the future.

You set up rules and blockades, creating an imaginary world.

You believe that world so strongly that you make it so!

If you cannot be aware of your own mind running rampant,

you cannot be aware of the results of your behavior.

Think before you act—but first, and most importantly,

notice what you think.

Make your thinking your first priority.

It is your baseline for making anything, in fact everything, better.

NAVIGATING AND ASSISTING IN THE AWAKENING OF HUMANITY

ALL ANIMALS

On Caring for Your Changing Bodies
as You Evolve

All of us are here because these are Universal messages—

Time is speeding up—we animals all feel it.

Physical bodies are changing as a result.

That is why you may be feeling pain or having health issues.

Grounding mechanisms are being challenged,

so work to stabilize yourselves.

Now more than ever, go outside into Nature.

It is fine—even required—to be more still

and stop exercise at times.

Your body will not suffer.

Listen to your bodies, do not force.

We know this is a challenge, but your bodies

are being energetically altered

so that you can withstand and sail through upcoming

and ongoing changes.

You are becoming vessels of light.

Continued...

Let go of what you think you know as truth about the body

and its treatment.

What matters is clean and whole.

Forget labels. They are all lies.

We know this is not an easy transition, but you can do it.

Go slowly. Rest often.

ALL ANIMALS

If You're a Sensitive, Protect Your Energy Field

If extreme emotions run through you that seem unrelated

to your personal experience,

it is because you are releasing trauma experienced by everyone,

including you.

Society's confusion, anger, anxiety, grief, frustration, and more

are passing through you

and may seem to turn off and on like a light switch.

We animals knew this would happen,

given the unrest around you.

If this is your experience, your sensitivity

is greater than you know—

similar to ours but with human levels of biology and chemicals

that have been thrown awry.

Daily energy work to protect and strengthen your energy field

is critical.

To enable energies to flow and not get trapped within,

envision an outlet above and below you.

ALL ANIMALS

You Are Shedding What Doesn't Serve You

We understand the cycles and changes that you and the Earth

are going through.

Nothing is what it seems, so step back and watch for a while.

If a situation or person confuses you or compromises

you in any way, step away and observe.

It is to be expected that everything you thought you

wanted or needed

no longer fits with the version of you that is emerging,

nor what you are awakening to.

The hardest part is how you feel before the changes solidify.

It will get easier.

ALL ANIMALS

You Are a Magnet for Others Who Are Awakening

When your attention is directed to all that helps,

heals, and regenerates,

your conversations with others will mirror that.

You will discover how many are like you.

When one person reveals their truth,

it becomes safe for others to share their own.

ALL ANIMALS

When the Energy Around You
Is Especially Challenging

We animals do not have the same expectations of ourselves

that you do.

Energy is our first priority, not accomplishments.

The quality of the energy determines the quality of outcomes.

That means working with compromised energy around you

creates problems.

Not everyone feels this but for sensitive folks who do,

dial it down,

and switch your work to another day, if need be.

ALL ANIMALS

The Body and Spirit Need a
Rest from Each Other

When you need to recharge, you can do what we do

—sleep more.

Sleep allows the time for the body to heal

and the spirit to be free.

The body and spirit benefit by having a break from one other,

like any relationship.

ALL ANIMALS

Expect the Waves! You Are Not Going Backwards

Shifts in consciousness come in waves.

It is natural to have ebbs and flows in your awareness.

Ebbs and flows do not mean you are going backwards.

You are integrating halos of consciousness

into your being and behavior.

Putting wisdom into practice takes time, repetition,

and patience with Self.

ALL ANIMALS

Signs That You Are Growing

When you catch yourself and notice how unpleasant you feel

if you slip into judgment, anger, or reactivity of any sort…

When you look upon other humans with compassion,

not intolerance…

When you make an effort to live 'softer' and stress less…

These are all signs of your growth.

BIRDS

On What They See Now, As Humans Awaken

We fly over ships and seas, covering vast distances

with few humans in sight,

and we can feel their disharmony from far off.

However, we are now seeing a tide of change for the better.

In every country, the light within is being turned on,

shining brighter and brighter.

It is so much greater than what you see from your vantage point.

There are many people waking up.

Please do not lose hope—the picture of what is unfolding

is more beautiful than you know.

It is just as we knew it would be.

BIRDS

Every Thought, Prayer, and Intention
Makes a Difference

Many people do not even know that they are changing this planet

for the better

with every thought, prayer, meditation, intention,

and loving action.

In the churches, in the schools their influence is felt—

across religions, countries, genders, races and generations.

We birds know because we are the global communication system.

We receive—and spread across the globe—

the word about the millions upon millions of people

who are not on TV and are not talked about.

It is important that you know how important

you and your inner being are

instead of evaluating yourself by outer actions only,

as you tend to do.

BIRDS

You Are Helping to Bring Balance to Earth

We realize it is not a comfortable time for many of you now,

even if your basic external circumstances look fine.

We feel your hearts and we know that many of you are jumpy,

sad, irritable, have problems sleeping, and feel lost

and disconnected 'for no reason.'

We have known for lifetimes that these Earth changes

have been coming.

You who are here now are bringing into balance

what was thrown off by so many who preceded you.

Take your cues from us to make it through all this.

Slow down and back off your routine.

Cocoon and recharge.

Turn to Nature for peace.

ELEPHANT
(MATRIARCH)

Watch the Play Unfold and Retain Your Autonomy

The complexities of human society are beginning to unravel.

Things that cause people fear and pain—like corruption —

will continue to break open and dissolve.

Ultimately, there will be a return to greater simplicity—

simple ways of being that work for all.

Do not get caught up in opinions, yours or others.

They can be very disruptive to health and happiness.

They are also inconsequential.

Step back and watch the play without letting it affect you.

See yourselves as separate from what takes place on the stage.

Those of you who are afraid give up your power

and will suffer the most.

Retain your heart-centeredness and you will not lose

your freedom or autonomy.

Your heart is the key to your power.

Put your hands over it daily as a reminder

that love will be the victor.

ELEPHANT
(MATRIARCH)

When Soul Growth Is Your Priority, Your Experience Changes

For those of you experiencing the awakening profoundly,

for whom so many human activities have lost their importance,

we want to reveal the following:

your Higher Selves see through the veil,

so what you thought you needed,

or what you believed were fundamental necessities of life,

may now play only a small role, not a starring one.

This could be a partner who is not your mate in Spirit

or things or experiences that don't serve you.

Performing or functioning in sync with unawakened humans

may feel as if you are acting in a play.

Your soul growth has become the most important thing to you,

and you are seeing with clear eyes.

Continued...

To all of this we say bravo,

even if you feel sick, flustered, depressed, out of sorts,

or out of place around other humans.

Go back into Nature and be with those who see—

and for whom the veil has never existed.

GIRAFFE

Open Your Eyes to the Light in Others

There are pockets of awakening everywhere,

even in the most unlikely of personalities.

You must open your eyes to the light in people around you.

Do not automatically write off those whom you assume

cannot understand.

Meet them where they are conversationally.

Remain heart-centered and you will open the door

to the beauty within them

and the common ground you share.

HORSE
(HUGO)

The Human Awakening Is Helping Animals Do Healing Work

Increasing numbers of horses are working in the healing fields.

And even more good is materializing on the energetic level.

As human awakening expands, blocks dissolve,

and this process affects us in a positive way.

There are now thinnings and holes

in the dense walls of human beliefs.

Now, behind the scenes, we are able to step into our power.

All positive changes expand outwards

and thus have a greater impact than you think.

HORSE
(JONO)
Human Thoughts Are Shifting

The mess you humans are in started so long ago,

that all of you living today are doing some mighty heavy lifting.

Every break you take away from 'automatic living'

helps you chip away at the clay around you.

We have faith in you.

We see the glimmers of awareness,

the private 'aha's' across millions of you.

We applaud you every time you shed a false belief or walk away

from what hurts, limits you or doesn't serve your wholeness.

We feel the tidal movement of your thoughts shifting

from treacherous,

to smooth, calm, and healing.

As you practice, the quality of your thoughts will shift towards

truth, harmony and 'Isness'

—the space where we live.

HORSE

(JONO)

To Evolve, Step Away from Mass-messaging

The most important thing is to step out of the fray—

the mass events, media, and messaging.

Mass consciousness shifts on a person by person basis,

until a tipping point is reached,

but you cannot shift when you are on autopilot.

Step away from the fray and let your own ideas

come from oneness with your heart.

LEOPARD

On Big Energetic Changes Afoot

There is still so much you do not know

about the causes of what is happening—and the why.

Big energy is descending—bigger than you can imagine.

It will uproot all the old ways of being on this planet.

The animals all know this, so they remain loosely tied to what is,

including their bodies—which you see as dense—

but they are not.

We see much further down the path where the understanding

that all Consciousness is one

becomes the experience for all.

LION

Two Simple Principles to Navigate This Changing World

The route to your solutions is short.

Just two simple principles will change your experience—

and the world's.

You do not have to make things so complicated.

SLOW DOWN.

DROP INTO KINDNESS.

REQUESTS FROM
THE ANIMAL KINGDOM

BEAR

Make Time for Contemplation
to Stop the Burn Out

You humans never know how to rest and then you wonder why

you burn out.

Animals innately know to stop, walk slowly, and contemplate.

We do it all the time—just watch us.

Why don't you humans get with the program?

Yes, you are guilty of 'do-ism.'

Your cells cannot regenerate if your switch is always on.

BIRDS

Notice Us to Keep Things in Perspective

When we sing, we ask you to look up.

Take one moment to breathe, feel joy,

and see the beauty of the sky that is always there

watching over you.

We wish you could feel what we feel,

the freedom of flight and what it means to soar.

We look down and see how small everything really is—

in comparison to the vastness of what is above.

Consider this perspective when you deal with problems

you think are so immense.

BIRDS

Take Care of Yourselves by Receiving from Nature

You humans need to take better care of yourselves,

even though you find it easier to care for others.

You are always about output e.g. even gratitude is output,

but you are not so skilled at receiving input!

You must allow yourselves to stop and savor.

Receive the energy and love that is all around you.

All non-human animals do this.

BLUE WHALE

Be Kinder to Yourselves

If we had one message, it would be to ask humans

to be kinder to themselves.

All healing stems from this principle.

Respect starts here. Even joy begins here.

Self-care is not a chore.

Think of how good you feel when you treat your body with love.

If you love and care for yourselves more,

by extension, it will be easier to do the same for your world.

BUFO TOAD

Please Treat All Beings with Compassion

We are misunderstood, just like many humans whom you judge

from the outside.

We serve to teach caution, as every species must embrace this

for survival,

including the pets you love and care for so dearly.

We mean no harm to anyone; we are gentle and peaceful.

We just contain a device that teaches harsh lessons.

We were given this part of ourselves by the Creator,

but we would not choose for it to be this way.

What our souls chose, our hearts did not.

We beg of all of you—stop sending us so much hatred.

It is painful.

Remember, you could be us.

We ask you to please treat us—and all beings—with compassion.

CAT
(COOKIE)

Take a Lesson from Feline Wisdom

All cats, domestic and wild, understand power, observation,

focus, and patience.

Because some of us are partnering with humans in this lifetime,

we are here to help you reclaim your power

through focused attention

and by separating yourself from the incessant chatter

of your mind.

Notice where your mind has gone when we stare you down.

You would all do well to learn from our example.

DOG
(MISTER T)
Follow Our Simple Ways to Be Happy

We keep trying to show you simpler ways—

things that, if you do them, will help you feel better and happier.

Smile when you are outside.

Notice the beauty in the smallest details.

Use your senses to their fullest extent.

Take your time.

DOG
(MISTER T)

Accept That You Need Each Other

When we walk you up to other people walking dogs,

we are not just greeting their dog!

We are also connecting humans with each other.

We are trying to make it easier for you to come together

because you isolate yourselves in your houses and get lonely.

You never have to be lonely.

You always have us and God and each other, if you just allow it,

and understand it is the way things should be.

We all need each other—plants, animals, and people.

DONKEY
(ELSA)

Tune into How You Feel Wherever You Go

Where you go matters, now more than ever.

You must check in always and notice if your heart, stomach,

throat, or head hurts or feels tight

when you enter a certain space.

Healing places make you feel flowing, calm, happy,

and loose in your body.

Notice how all your tight and aching parts feel

when you are in a healing space.

Pay more attention to how you feel

as you move from place to place.

ELEPHANT

Publicize the Good, As Opposed to Fighting 'Evil'

Let go of your addiction to fighting against 'evil.'

We know this is perhaps the most challenging task of all,

but you are feeding the suffering you dwell upon.

Put your attention on what is possible,

not on acts of human greed.

Set aside time each day to see all that you want for yourselves,

for animals, and Mother Earth.

There is much more going on to bring this world

to its rightful place of health and wholeness.

Concern yourself only with those efforts and your own energies.

Publicize all the good that is being done,

so it will keep growing like a weed.

ELEPHANT

Send Love to Every Situation Possible

Step back and allow others to grow at their own pace.

You cannot rush the process.

Instead, send love to every situation and see renewal in its wake.

We know humans are not having an easy time now.

Everything is being brought out into the light

and the changes can rock your sense of reality.

You must know that the animals are with you—

grateful and cheering you on in your efforts

to live authentically, find joy, and release the programming

and the painful, faulty beliefs

that have held you back until now.

Keep going, all of you.

Please keep your faith—we need it.

HORSE
(CARBON)

Slowing Down Helps You and Others

Rushing erodes the energy of your nervous system.

It even blocks wisdom from emerging from within you.

When you slow down,

your heart relaxes and your mind clears.

Your energy field, which impacts others, becomes clear as a pool.

Your voice becomes more soothing.

People gravitate to you and want to listen to what you have to say.

HORSE
(HONEYBEE)

Simplify Your Life So You Can Focus on Harmony

Cut out the non-essential.

Simplify your life and your habits as much as possible

to live and breathe the creation you desire.

It is enough to focus on breath and intention

and seeing the world born of love and harmony.

Pay closer attention to the energy of each person you meet.

Notice how their energy affects you.

Embrace every single one of them with love,

compassion, and acceptance.

They have all been wounded and misguided by programming,

just as you have.

HORSE

(HUGO)

Call Us in When You Set Intention

No one can just work alone anymore.

Energetic power grows immensely when combined.

When you set an intention for the good—for harmony, peace,

and love—energetically call us in.

We await the opportunity to work with those of you

who understand that everything begins and ends with energy—

and that all change happens from this level.

LIONS
(MALE AND FEMALE)
Use Fierceness as the Sacred Tool It Is

Humans vastly misunderstand the purpose of being fierce.

They use it to minimize others, to control, and to express rage.

We do not dominate for the sake of power.

We have a much deeper purpose.

You see us roar—yes, we possess great energetic strength—

but you do not see how we use it in our world.

What you see with your eyes is not what counts.

You must look beneath the surface.

The true purpose of fierceness is to keep things in balance—

to stand for what is right and just.

It is to keep Ego where it belongs, as a servant

to the greater good of all.

Ego must be kept in check, not beaten down.

Fierceness is a sacred tool to be used with wisdom.

Tap into your own ferocity to overcome challenges within you.

Think about it.

MOUSE

Understand That Every Occurrence
Is for Your Soul Growth

Most humans still cannot comprehend that there is

a reason for everything,

that there is no such thing as an accident,

no matter how shocking or incomprehensible an event

or circumstance may be.

Soul growth—of the individual and the collective—

is the main purpose behind abuse, cruelty, shock,

and other experiences difficult to comprehend.

Growth can be painful and often does not occur

until the most extreme consequence of ignorance is reached.

PYTHON

Remember the Importance of Respect

We have a high level of respect in the animal world.

Turning your human world around means reclaiming this pillar

of life that you seem to have lost.

Give your full attention when another is speaking.

Honor your commitments.

Show kindness and manners on the roads,

in your homes, and offices.

Watch how the quality of behavior around you rises,

as you implement these basic principles

It begins with you.

SACRED COW

Bring a Different Focus to Doing Business

It requires deep thinking and caring to change the way

that money, which is energy,

can be generated without harm.

Loving intention needs to enter corporate thinking.

Honesty and integrity are the key drivers of the New Business.

The people who drive these companies will feel better, will thrive,

and will be more successful

because collaborators and clients will step up and join them

in ventures that are both profitable and good for all.

SQUIRREL

Remember Your Own Power and Be Proud

Stop being so intimidated by big things,

like governments and corporations.

Walk with your heads held high.

Pride is not a bad thing; it just gets a bad rap.

People who take pride in things—their bodies, their homes,

their property, their neighborhoods—

take care of them and don't pollute and destroy them!

Just this one concept, if you could put it into practice,

could change society as you know it.

SQUIRREL

Slow Down to Upgrade Your Actions

People don't realize their biggest problem is that they never

slow down.

If they did, they'd make better decisions,

say nicer things they don't regret,

and get more answers to questions and problems.

Heck, it's like numero uno.

SPIRIT:
How to Invite It
into Your Daily Life

ALL ANIMALS

Pay Attention to Signs So
Spirit Can Come Through

Many of you now have the opportunity to tap into your

multi-dimensional nature,

and receive wisdom and insights from Spirit.

You may be unaware

that you are missing the signs urging you to stop

and allow Spirit to speak to you and through you.

If, out of nowhere, you feel hit by intense sleepiness, stop.

Sit. Listen. See. Sense. Feel. Know.

Grab a pen and write it all down.

Get to know you and your incredible capabilities.

GORILLA

Partner with Spirit Every Day

In all you do, first ask for help.

Ask of guides, angels, God, the universe—

whatever you believe in.

You are never alone and all the greatest achievements

—personal and global—

are created through partnership with those not trapped in

the human condition.

HORSE

Give in to 'Isness' to Welcome the Presence of Spirit

How to experience Spirit?

Give in to the 'Isness' of things—the truth, the rightness

that breathes there,

just beneath the surface of the tension haze you know as reality.

It is so much faster and easier than you imagine it to be.

It is simply, consciously, telling the mind to hush

so that Spirit can speak.

The more you embrace 'Isness,' the more you will feel a melting

inside your heart,

as you come back to the never-ending welcome that awaits you.

HORSE
(HUGO)

The Love and Energy Available
from Spirit Are Limitless

Partnership with Spirit means you never have to worry

about asking for too much help.

Trying to go it alone is a major and massive human mistake.

Stop.

We animals always look to Spirit (aka 'God', 'The All', 'All That Is')

for help.

We never have issues of guilt or worry

that we are asking too much.

The supply of love and energy is limitless.

You limit yourselves by not tapping into it.

LEOPARD

Switch from Doing to Receiving Mode

The way out is to go in.

The answer to 'what to do?' is to stop.

Train yourself to allow for a change.

When you are in 'do mode,' you block guidance from us,

from your Higher Selves, and from Spirit.

Change your switch to receive mode.

If your slate is never clear, how can Spirit write upon it?

You may think that this is inaction but it is not.

It is a very different kind of action.

It is the energetic fabric of the Earth Mother herself.

MOOSE

You Are Already Holy in the Eyes of God/Spirit

I am here to talk to you about being in a state of Grace.

Contrary to what you may believe, Grace is not connected

to gratitude—but it may cause it!

Feeling Grace means you are already made holy by God.

You humans are so focused on your own 'sin' and 'wrongdoing'

that you cannot imagine this truth.

If you could see yourselves this way, as I do,

perhaps you would feel some relief and ease.

You might also, unknowingly, raise the quality of your behavior

to match this understanding.

If you are holy in the eyes of God, ask yourself

'what would a holy man or woman do?'

Meet us, the animals, here in this place of pure knowingness

that you are already made holy by God.

Contemplate this for a while.

SEAL

Practice Talking to Spirit

It is perhaps easier for us than for humans,

as our heads don't block us from experiencing Spirit

in any moment.

Spirit is everywhere and it is in you as well,

but you can only experience it by escaping

the confines of your brains.

You can each feel it in your own ways

through your individual gifts.

Some will feel it in the body, others see images,

sense, or hear things.

For us, it is the doubtless knowing that "The Greater"

is always with us, guiding what is to be.

It is so comforting.

We know you struggle with this and doubt so very much.

Practice the knowing that your Greater is always there to turn to.

Talk to it. Practice your experience of communion with it.

As you become comfortable with the knowing,

and speak it to yourself,

it will become your reality.

Acknowledgments and Deepest Gratitude to:

Andrea Gaines for your loving and empowering support through the best and the worst of times. You set a high bar for the New Earth.

Christine Hendler for your breathtaking heart and vision, creating a new paradigm for harmony with our fellow beings.

Deana Riddle for your even-keeled expertise that transforms every manuscript into something beautiful.

Dorothea Lowe for your powerful knowing, positivity, and consistent commitment to sharing the animals' wisdom with the world. You astound me.

Farlish Mohamed for creating the face of *We Walk Beside You* with your beautiful images.

Laura Sodders for your incredible friendship, and "whatever is needed" attitude; you are always sewing threads of goodness and connection so that everyone benefits.

Vanessa Park for your editing expertise, clarity and professionalism. It's a joy to work with you.

Every animal soul and consciousness, I bow to you in wonder and humility for continuing to allow me into your world and consistently reminding me that I've barely scratched the surface.

And to Mom, Carol Calvert, Penny Meno, Jessalynn Taker, and Mister T for loving me through all of my humanness. You all deserve wings.

Photo Credits and Many Thanks to:

Page 17: Photo of Britnie Banks with Red at Horse, Heart & Connection, Ojai, California. Founded and directed by Andrea Gaines, Horse, Heart & Connection provides a unique equine experience where visitors explore mindfulness and nonverbal communication, and cultivate intuition with the horse as their mirror. Learn more and contact Andrea at: www.horseheartandconnection.com or Instagram: @horseheartandconnection.

Page 146: Photo of Lovebug by Kim Harrington, Animal Reiki teacher with the Shelter Animal Reiki Association (SARA), a non-profit organization that teaches and promotes the Let Animals Lead® method created by Kathleen Prasad of Animal Reiki Source, using meditation practices to bring peace and wellness to shelter animals. Kim is also the founder of mindovermatterreiki.com.

Page 155: Selvynna (pictured with Teddy) challenges the notion that all cats belong in the house, as she and Teddy travel far and wide, side by side. Follow their adventures on Instagram: @theoretically.teddy.

Printed in Great Britain
by Amazon